LIVING
WITH
OUTRAGEOUS JOY

Also by Madeleine Kay

Living Serendipitously . . . keeping the wonder alive

Coming soon

How Will I Ever Get Over My Happy Childhood
(Stories)

LIVING

WITH

OUTRAGEOUS JOY

MADELEINE KAY

CHRYSALIS PUBLISHING
P.O. Box 675
Flat Rock, NC 28731
www.chrysalispublishing.net

Second Printing

ISBN 13: 978-0-9715572-4-6
ISBN 10: 0-9715572-4-1

Printed in the United States of America
10 9 8 7 6 5 4 3 2

DEDicatiON

To Life —
this crazy, wonderful adventure
with all
its mystery, wonder and surprises.
Le Chiam . . .

I believe in grabbing at Life.
Every minute a new minute.
Every second a new second
. . . never happened before.

Zorba the Greek
Nikos Kazantzakis

Life is meant to be enjoyed, life is meant to be easy — Give yourself permission to be happy, to laugh, to succeed, to have everything you want — right here and right now.

Life is fun — EnjOy it —
Savor it . . . Live it.

As a demonstration of your commitment to living every day with joy, please go to www.madeleinekay.com/LWOJ and sign up to download your free personalized certificate of commitment commemorating and celebrating your decisive first step.

PERSONAL COMMITMENT TO JOY

I, _____, give myself
permission to live, laugh and love my life.
I will work like I don't need the money,
   sing like no one is listening,
      dance like no one is watching,
         laugh like I mean it
            and love like I've never been hurt.
I commit to savoring each moment . . . and really
   enjoying my life.

_____   _____
       Signed   Dated

fORWaRD

Joy is contagious ... joy is what every one of us wants to feel more of in our lives.

This charming little gift book will re-ignite that feeling of joy in your life and your passion for living. Playfully inspiring and motivating, this unique collection of insights, sayings and quotes will delight and revitalize you. It will open you up to the joy and adventure of living your life to the fullest every single day ... unleashing in you that feeling of *aliveness* that so many of us are longing to feel.

This book will truly get you to live your life as though ~~Anything~~ Everything Is Possible!

Maggie Duke, President
Duke Enterprises

A NOTE FROM THE AUTHOR

There are 18 keys to living with outrageous joy. Why 18? Because in many ancient languages there were no numbers, so the letters had numerical equivalents. In ancient Hebrew, the word for Life is *Chai*. Made up of two letters – a *chet* and a *yod* – the numerical equivalent of *Chai* is 18.

Also, in Numerology, the ancient study of the mystical significance of numbers, the number 9 signifies completion . . . and 18 – 1 plus 8 – equals 9.

I don't think it's any accident, but rather quite serendipitous that 18 therefore means life, vitality and aliveness that are complete and whole.

For maximum benefit, I suggest you read this book through once and then read one key each day . . .

making it your own for that day by simply being aware of it. You do not need to do, practice, remember or work at anything. Simply be aware and let the words flow through you for that day. Make this a life-long habit . . . and see how outrageous joy begins to permeate your life.

There are only two things you can give your children,
and they are roots and wings.

Peggy Noonan

INTRODUCTION

The greater danger for most of us
lies not in setting our aim
too high and falling short;
but in setting our aim too low
and achieving our mark.

Michelangelo

Be fully present
in all you say and do.
This immediacy makes it possible
for you to feel that aliveness all of us
are craving and longing to feel.

Live your life
as though everything is a miracle –
with the belief
that at any moment
something wonderful is about to happen.
When you live this way,
wonderful things do happen
because you are inviting them into your life.

Always be honest with yourself.
This is the basis
for wholeness and integrity . . .
for self-awareness and self-discovery . . .
to knowing who you are
and how you can contribute to this world.

Part 1

ROOTS

I

LiKE YOURSELf

You yourself, as much as anybody
in the entire universe, deserve
your love and appreciation.

Buddha

Treat yourself
with the same kindness and generosity of spirit
as you would your best friend . . .
in how you speak about yourself,
talk to yourself
and the advice you give yourself.

Know yourself.
Be willing
to be totally and
brutally honest with yourself,
seeking, rather than what you want to hear
. . . the truth.

Compliment and congratulate yourself
just as you would a friend,
whenever you say
or do something
significant, wise, gracious or kind.
Openly appreciating yourself in this way
enables you to really
appreciate and compliment others.

Practice the art of self-love.
Loving yourself
        and being kind and generous to yourself
            is not selfish . . .
        It is a way of
                replenishing,
            revitalizing,
                rewarding
        and restoring
the balance, beauty and vitality inside you
        that you give to and share with others.

II

Claim joy as your Right

Do not postpone joy.

Source Unknown

Express joy in your daily life
whenever you can,
so that joy becomes a habit.
Cultivate the habit of living joyously
so that your very first response
to life's experiences,
like the tropism of a plant that turns naturally
towards the sun,
is one of joy.

Believe
that you can
do what you want in life . . .
Be an active dreamer,
who takes action on your dreams
because you believe in them
and know that everything is possible.

Live with joy and an open heart,
like a flower
      that does not seek out the bee
for its honey . . . It just opens up
   and receives.

III

WELCOME YOUR DRAGONS

Just as the hand, held before the eye,
can hide the tallest mountain,
so can the routine of everyday life
keep us from seeing
the vast radiance and the secret wonders
that fill the world.

Chasidic, 18th Century

Appreciate and know
that you are a work of art . . .
and that each person is.
We are all a work in progress
. . . a canvas
upon which we are continually painting.

Accept everyone, including yourself,
without judgment.
We are all doing the best we can.
If we knew how
to do or be any better,
we would.

Always be kind . . .
Remember the fairy tales of old
 in which the kindness, love,
trust and non-judgment
 of the "fair maiden"
transforms the scary, fiery, ugly dragon
 into a handsome prince, who it turns out,
was merely under some "evil" spell.
     Be the one
who breaks the spell of "evil" over others
 with your kindness, compassion, love and
understanding.

See and embrace
the opportunity, lesson and gift
in every situation
. . . no matter how difficult or painful it
may appear.
Accepting and embracing
your pain, suffering and difficulties,
allows them to move through you
so you can become happy and whole again.

IV

CREATE PORTABLE ROOTS

*You cannot discover new oceans
unless you have the courage
to lose sight of the shore.*

Source Unknown

Interweave your freedom with security
and your security with your freedom.
Security is not tied to a
person, place or situation,
and freedom comes from knowing
who you are
and living according to the integrity
of that truth.

Savor and enjoy possibility living.
Respond to the call
of life's high adventure
by demystifying risk-taking
and making it exciting.

Accomplish more with less effort –
When you harness
the forces of harmony, joy and love
you create
success and good fortune with
effortless ease.

V

EXPLORE YOUR UNLIMITED
POSSIBILITIES

Life is either a daring adventure
Or nothing . . .

Helen Keller

Transform your dreams into reality
by believing that anything . . . no,
everything is possible.
Making choices and decisions
and acting on them,
moves your dreams
from the realm of the abstract
to the realm
of the concrete and the possible.

Embrace the unknown
as an exciting adventure – a gift
or a present
being laid at your feet
. . . waiting for you to open it.

Say a resounding YES to Life!
    Words are very powerful
triggers – so choose your
    words carefully, as
carefully as you do your friends;
    for the words you live with
        can ultimately be your
    best friends.

VI

DISCOVER YOUR CONSISTENCY IN PASSION

A foolish consistency is the hobgoblin of little minds.

Ralph Waldo Emerson

Develop and foster a flexibility
and curiosity that
enable and encourage you to
change, adapt and grow;
so that like a snake
that periodically sheds its
old skin, you leave
behind that which no longer
contributes to your continued
growth and development.

fertilize your imagination
so you are continually giving birth
to new parts of yourself.

Be stimulated by
and trust your passion . . . let it lead you.
Your passion
is your true and unwavering guide that,
like a compass, will direct
you to whatever and wherever
you need to go with
energy, focus and commitment.

VII

just let go

*Trying creates impossibilities,
letting go creates what is desired.*

Stalking Wolf, Apache Elder

Let go and release
your resistance.
Since what you resist persists . . .
the energy of
acceptance
helps things move and
flow through you,
resolving themselves.

Quiet your mind and be still.
Like a stone
tossed into a lake causes
ripples and often churns up mud,
our chatterbox mind clutters
our thoughts and emotions.
Like a lake that
becomes still and clear
once the stone settles on the
bottom of the lake, our minds
become clear when we are
still and let go.

focus your attention on
what you want,
not on what you do not want.
The world is a mirror,
reflecting back to us what
we put out there –
attracting into our life
that on which we dwell.

VIII

LISTEN TO

YOUR INTUITION

Remember –
The Force will be with you always . . .

Obi-Wan "Ben" Kanobi / *Star Wars*
George Lucas

Trust your intuition
and learn to listen to it.
Intuition is
the Voice of God.
It is our inner guide
gently and subtlely directing us
to all that we need and desire.

Rejoice in knowing
that there is an underlying order
in the world . . .
that life is not random and chaotic,
but rather is governed by natural laws
. . . a universal consciousness, a cosmic force,
a Logos,
as the Greeks called it.

Develop and nurture your
intuition by beginning with
small things – so you
build a confidence and a trust and
develop the habit of listening
to and hearing your intuition –
that still, small voice
inside you . . . or that feeling
in your gut.

IX

CHOOSE HAPPINESS

*People are usually as happy as
they make up their minds to be . . .*

Abraham Lincoln

Choose
     what kind of human being
  you want to be, and then
          be it.
     Decide
  what kind of life
    you want to live and then
         live it.

Smile a lot...
Send messages
of happiness
to your body and your
psyche, by smiling
and laughing often.

Appreciate
how happy you can be
~ NOW ~
Happiness is not something you have to earn.
It is your birthright.
Claim it.

X

LiVE ABuNDƏNTLY

*Not what we have But
what we enjoy,
constitutes our abundance.*

Epicurus

Use your "good" dishes,
wear your favorite clothes,
entertain in your living room,
treat yourself to gourmet delights.
Affirm
that you are rich
by
Living richly.

give out of abundance ~
Give
graciously, whole-heartedly
and happily.
Give all that you can . . .
compliments, time, money, compassion
and see your riches multiply.

Enter the cycle of nature –
the ebb and flow,
the give and take,
the movement into and out of.
In nature, the outflow creates
the inflow in one continuous
movement,
bringing back to us
that which we give out –
enriching our lives.

XI

INDULGE IN
ACTIVE GRATITUDE

*If the only prayer you said in your life
was "thank you;"
that would suffice.*

Meister Eckhart

Be the magnet
for rejoicing and thanksgiving.
Gratitude
attracts to you more
of what you are grateful for.
Active gratitude is
a natural response
to living abundantly.

Notice and marvel
at
the small beauties
and
gifts in your life.
When you do,
you become an active participant
in life
and one with all of Life.

Live gratitude.
Breathe gratitude.
Celebrate gratitude.
How you live
each day of your life
IS
your Life.
Live each day with
appreciation.

Part II

WINGS

XII

DARE TO DREAM

What you can do, or dream you can, do it,
Boldness has genius, power, and magic in it.

Johann Wolfgang von Goethe

Dream Big...
   Dream often...
   And
      Just Do it!

Remember, anything . . . no . . .
Everything
         is possible.

Respect your dreams,
Listen to your dreams,
         Believe in your dreams
Act on your dreams.

Know this . . .
In your dreams
is your power
and your strength;
Your dreams come
from the energy source –
the core of who you are –
Your soul.

XIII

Exult the magic of Believing

They can because they think they can.

Virgil

Mobilize
the inner and outer forces
that will enable you
to achieve your goals . . .
Just Believe.

Anchor your belief
in trust and faith, in a universe
that treats us kindly
and with love –

a universe
that is
always on our side.

Replace "what if's"
with "sure, why nots."
Operate from a belief
system that
already sees
the fait accompli.

Couple
your deep, firm,
  unwavering belief
in yourself, your dreams and
  the possible
with passion.
    Belief coupled with passion
guarantees success.

XIV

PURSUE YOUR PASSION

CHANCES

aren't given. They're taken.

Source Unknown

Get excited!
Enthusiasm is contagious,
even to and within
yourself.
Let the sparks
of passion fly
and
set you on fire.

Unleash your passion.
Passion
makes you bold and
willing
to take risks for
what you believe in.

Expand and open your senses.
They are your receptors
to the outside world –
They alert you
to the new opportunities,
miracles and synchronicities
that serendipitously
arise
when you awaken
and
follow your passion.

XV

EXPECT THE BEST

*Treat someone as if they are
what they could become,
and that is what
one day they shall be.*

Johann Wolfgang von Goethe

Expect to succeed,
to get what you desire
to accomplish what you hope for,
to feel how you want to feel.
See it, feel it, hear it, taste it,
touch it,
so it is palpable,
concrete and real.

Raise your expectations.
Your expectations
usually determine
what you will
receive
and
achieve.

Accept
and be willing
to receive Life's best,
and then
get out of your own way
and let it happen.

XVI

LiVE aS if

Try not – Do or do not …
   There is no try.

Yoda / The Empire Strikes Back
   George Lucas

Act as though
you already
are or have all that you desire.
This coaxes and allows the "if" to
slip away . . .
leaving only "when."

Living as if
creates a momentum
and an energy
that move you beyond
doubt, fear and worry –
Living as if
liberates your energy, time and resources
to do, be and have
what you want
and to live
as you wish.

Stand confidently and
be willing to announce to the
     world, God and yourself that
You are loved
     You are worthy
You are rich, successful and happy . . .
     Knowing that this is what
God, the Universe,
     The Force, the Universal Spirit
want for you –
     Your Happiness . . . Your Success . . .
          Your Well-Being.

XVII

FIND YOUR ANSWERS
IN LOVE

This is Love: to fly toward a secret sky,
to cause a hundred veils to fall each moment.
First to let go of life.
Finally, to take a step without feet.

Rumi

Become Love . . .
Become permeated by and
suffused with Love
so that – like looking at life
through rose-colored glasses,
you see only the beauty,
the softness, the melding together
of everything and
everyone in
the universe
as one.

Empty yourself . . .
Forgive
        yourself and others
for not being perfect.
        Then fill yourself up . . .
    Surrender to Love – the ultimate
letting go
        . . . the ultimate acceptance.

Love yourself.
Love does not see faults and blemishes.
Love sees
only the good – Like looking
through a filtered lens.
So
Love transforms
– powerfully, completely and ineluctably –
both the person loved
and the person doing the loving.

XVIII

LIVE SERENDIPITOUSLY

The child is the father of man.

William Wordsworth

Explore the aliveness
of child-mind.
    Child-mind that is beautiful and
wise in its purity and clarity.
        Child-mind that is unmuddled,
direct, intense, playful and immediate.
            Child-mind that is organic and
kinetic, still and focused.
                Child-mind that is
        me and all
            at the same time.

Revel in the moment.
Seize the Day.
~ Carpe Diem ~
Respond to the call to
take action
in your life,
to experience the moment,
Enjoy "now."
This moment
is all we have,
all that is real,
all that we can
change, affect or influence.

foster a sense of mystery,
a sense of wonder and awe –
a responsiveness to life's serendipities.

Discover the yin and the yang
of child-mind:
   The wisdom and strength
   of its simplicity.
Simplicity –
   a thing distilled down to its essence,
its core . . . where
   the truth, beauty and power of a thing
always resides.

THE 18 KEYS TO LIVING WITH OUTRAGEOUS JOY

I

Like Yourself

II

Claim Joy as Your Right

III

Welcome Your Dragons

IV

Create Portable Roots

V

Explore Your Unlimited Possibilities

VI

Discover Your Consistency in Passion

VII

Just Let Go

VIII

Listen to Your Intuition

IX

Choose Happiness

X

Live Abundantly

XI

Indulge in Active Gratitude

XII

Dare to Dream

XIII

Exult the Magic of Believing

XIV

Pursue Your Passion

XV

Expect the Best

XVI

Live As If

XVII

Find Your Answers in Love

XVIII

Live Serendipitously